The Prayer of Jabez

Fulfill Your Destiny

Emmanuel Asante

Ocala, FL

Copyright © 2018 Emmanuel Asante

All rights reserved. No part of this publication may be reproduced, distributed, or transmitted in any form or by any means, including photocopying, recording, or other electronic or mechanical methods, without the prior written permission of the publisher, except in the case of brief quotations embodied in critical reviews and certain other noncommercial uses permitted by copyright law. For permission requests, write to the publisher, addressed "Attention: Permissions Coordinator," at the address below.

Zeta Publishing, Inc
3850 SE 58th Ave
Ocala, FL 34480
www.zetapublishing.com

Ordering Information:
Quantity sales. Special discounts are available on quantity purchases by corporations, associations, and others. For details, contact the publisher at the address above.
Orders by U.S. trade bookstores and wholesalers. Please contact Zeta Publishing: Tel: (352) 694-2553; Fax: (352) 694-1791 or visit www.zetapublishing.com

ISBN: 978-1-947191-43-3 (sc)

ISBN: 978-1-947191-44-0 (e)

Library of Congress Control Number: 2017956380

Printed in the United States of America

Table of Contents

The Prayer of Jabez 1

Jabez called on the God of Israel 6

Bless Me Indeed 11

Enlarge My Coast 15

Your Hand Might Be With Me 18

Keep Me From Evil 21

That It May Not Grieve Me 24

God Granted Jabez's Request 29

Lessons from Jabez's Prayer 32

Solutions to Situations 36

Conclusion 54

Quiz Program 59

Introduction

Prayer in its simplest term is a communication with God. Talking and listening to God enables believers to pour their hearts out in words spontaneously. Prayer also enables believers to build relationship with God, hence, it is imperative for believers to "pray without ceasing." [1 Thessalonians 5:17]

Some believers are used to requesting for prayers on prayer hotlines or from Christian intercessory groups whenever they are in trouble in life. Although, it is a step in the right direction to solicit prayers from prayer hotlines, yet when you reach your crossroads like Jabez did, it is very significant to pray diligently to change your destiny for the better. The Lord Jesus said "But when you pray, go into your room and shut the door and pray to your father who is in secret. And your Father who sees in secret will reward you" [Matthew 6:6].

Jabez was a descendant of the tribe of Judah whose high distinction among his brothers seemed to have been manifested owing to his diligence in prayer.

Jabez instead of being born into the world with a silver spoon in his mouth was born with a proclamation of sorrow upon his life. However, Jabez defied his hopeless name and dysfunctional beginning and as a matter of urgency prayed earnestly for God to turn his situation around.

Jabez's encounter with the God of Israel is one of the greatest life changing prayer masterpieces to have been written in Scriptures which is worthy of emulation.

The prayer of Jabez has been outlined as a lesson text or a case study coupled with a well digested powerful prayer points to inculcate believers with the habit of praying. It will also help believers to reposition themselves to take their destiny into their own hands by crying out to God for a restoration. The Bible declares, "The effectual fervent prayer of a righteous man avails much" [James 5:16].

Furthermore, it is very essential to take a lesson from Jabez's story, a man who was nobody in his household but cried out to God for a change and suddenly, he was transformed to a more honorable status. Eventually, he became the head of a family of the tribe of Judah. The Bible declares, "He will call on me, and I will answer him; I will be with him in trouble, I will deliver him and honor him" [Psalms 91:15].

Again, the prayer of Jabez will give believers the hope that whatever curses might have influenced their blessings, when they take their destiny into their own hands and make an earnest appeal for restoration, God will surely grant them double for their trouble.

Above all, Jabez's experience will reshape believers to eschew negative confession and instead declare God's blessings over their children, their lives and their family as well. The Bible teaches us that "Life and death are in the power of the tongue, he who loves it will eat the fruit thereof." [Proverbs 18:21]. Therefore, I would like to encourage you to choose life by declaring God's Word into your circumstance as it will enlighten your path and make your way prosperous.

Dear reader, may the Good Lord richly bless you to fulfill your destiny and also to become a prayer warrior in this End-Time as you read this book.

Books used for references:

All Scriptures given in this Book are either from the King James Version or the New International Version.

Acknowledgment

I would like to acknowledge the valuable contributions some important people played in this book.

Their prayer support, time and professionalism helped me to put the puzzles together and gave it a big short. Rev. Chris Boache and Mr. Edmund Saarah-Mensah for their professionalism to edit the manuscripts was just incredible. To all my family members, especially my wife, Georgina, my children Linda, Rita, and Isaac Asante for their unflinching support when writing this book. To my beloved mother, Hannah Buansi, for her prayers.

Dedication

I would like to dedicate this book to the glory of God who gave me the strength to accomplish my vision.

I also like to dedicate this book to my fellow servants in Christ.

I am indebted to dedicate this book to God's chosen vessel, the late Evangelist, Francis Akwasi Amoako of blessed memory. The late Evangelist, Francis Amoako had the love and passion for intercessory prayers. Therefore, he established prayer towers across the spectrum to encourage believers to become prayer warriors.

As a result, Resurrection Power & Living Bread Ministries International has inculcated the habit of praying fervently. The late Evangelist, Amoako was an exceptional man of God whose specialty was demonology and spiritual warfare. Graciously, Jehovah God used him mightily across the regions of Ghana and beyond.

What's more? His powerful preaching coupled with his prophetic ministry has placed him in a very high pedestal. By the grace of God, many men of God had sprung out of his ministry of which I am so blessed to be one of them. Having been under his unique ministry for some time, the impartation has helped me to become an intercessor and to write this book. Therefore, God's chosen vessel, the late

Evangelist Francis Akwasi Amoako's legacy will be remembered from one generation to another.

Foreword

Prayer is the key to every successful Christian life, and (as stated in God's Word in James 5:16, "The effectual fervent prayer of a righteous man avails much"). It is with great honor that I write about this book on Jabez.

In reference to the Bible, through Genesis to Revelation, we find that God's means of communication has always been through prayer. It is also evident that God used men of prayer in many instances to accomplish what he intended to do. I have known Pastor Asante at the Resurrection Power and Living Bread Ministries for several years now. He is a dedicated and humble servant of God.

The story of the prayer of Jabez unveils the secrets of how God can change situations, and also serves as a reminder that there is nothing too hard for God. In the introduction of this book, he explains how God enables believers to pour their hearts out in words spontaneously to Him, and that means, in every situation of man's life God has activated a hot line in the form of prayer which as believers, we must take advantage of, to our benefit. (Jeremiah 33:3) New King James Version (NKJV) "Call to Me, and I will answer you, and show you great and mighty things, which you do not know."

The prayer of Jabez illustrates his fervent prayer to God that he might not suffer what his name implies. It was a very powerful prayer point which turned to change his destiny for the rest of his life.

Pastor Asante went further to outline some important prayer points, where Jabez called on the God of Israel, and said, bless me indeed, enlarge my coast and keep me from evil. The book is arranged in a way that is easy to read and understand. The book of Jabez discusses times of trouble, divine protection, divine guidance, deliverance, fear, family protection and many more.

As a man of prayer, myself, I am glad he has taken time to write this book which I love to read and would not hesitate to recommend to all interested readers as well.

Rev. Dr. Ebenezer Kyere Nkansah
[Senior Pastor] Hope of Glory Church, MD, USA

Chapter 1

The Prayer of Jabez

JABEZ PRAYER POINTS

"And Jabez was more honorable than his brethren: and his mother called his name Jabez: saying, because I bare him with sorrow. And Jabez called on the God of Israel: saying, Oh that you would bless me indeed, and enlarge my coast, and that thine hand might be with me, and that you would keep me from evil. that it may not grieve me. And God granted him that which he requested" [1 Chronicles 4:9-10 KJV].

Jabez was designated to be more honorable than his brothers but he did not experience the divine blessings God had bestowed on him initially. The reason behind it was the negative pronouncements made by his mother over him, saying, I gave birth to him in sorrow which became his name Jabez and which had a great impact on his life.

The Bible did not state whether Jabez's father had died earlier on given the reason for Jabez to be labeled with sorrow. Or his father was a dissolute and irresponsible who might have disappeared from the scene before Jabez was born.

Certainly, one can imagine that Jabez's mother's heart was filled with sorrow due to the pain that she experienced during the birth of her son. Following the delivery the mother named her son Jabez signifying sorrow. Coincidentally, the memory of Jabez's critical circumstance which marked his birth was perpetuated in his name.

Perhaps, Jabez grew up and discovered that he was not prospering but rather grieving in life because his name was drenched by sorrow. Presumably, after Jabez had found out the meaning behind his name to be "sorrow", he took his destiny into his own hands and cried out to God to avert it. During the encounter, he made some five powerful prayer points to tap into the supernatural blessings of God.

Fervently, Jabez prayed unto the Living God and said:

1. Bless me indeed,

2. Enlarge my coast,

3. Your hand might be with me,

4. Keep me from evil,

5. That it may not grief me and God granted his request.

God restored back his dignity and he was transformed to be named after a city called Jabesh-Gilead. [see ref1]

Geographically, Jabesh-Gilead was located in the eastern side of the Jordan River in Israel which featured prominently in the history of King Saul. His rescue of the people of Jabesh-Gilead from the Ammonites therefore marked the effective beginning of the Israelite monarchy. The Bible reminds us that. They told the messengers who had come, "Say to the men of Jabesh Gilead, By the time the sun is hot tomorrow, you will be rescued. When the messengers went and reported this to the men of Jabesh, they were elated" [1Samuel 11:9].

Years later, the people of Jabesh-Gilead never forgot this act of King Saul. Passionately, they also demonstrated the high regard in which they held King Saul by retrieving the bodies of the slain king and his sons at Gilboa. For it is written "And when all Jabesh-Gilead heard all that the Philistines had done to Saul, They arose, all the valiant men, and took away the body of Saul, and the bodies of his sons, and brought them to Jabesh, and buried their bones under the oak in Jabesh, and fasted seven days" [1Chronicles 10:11-12].

As a result, King David also expressed thanks to their brave deeds and eventually removed King Saul's bones from Jabesh-Gilead. The Bible declares "Then the men of Judah came, and there they anointed David king over the house of Judah. They told David: "It was the men of Jabesh-Gilead who buried Saul." David sent messengers to the men of Jabesh-Gilead and said to them, "The LORD bless you, because you have shown this kindness to Saul your lord when you buried him. Now, may the LORD show kindness and faithfulness to you, and I will also show the same goodness to you because you have done this deed. Therefore, be strong and courageous, for though Saul your lord is dead, the house of Judah has anointed me king over them." [2 Samuel 2:4-7]

Jabesh-Gilead was the city where the families of the scribes in Israel inhabited. In other words, Jabez's honorable character drew many scribes around him at Jabesh-Gilead which was named after him. The Bible reveals:

"And the clans of scribes who lived at Jabez: The Tirathites, Shimeathites and Sucathites. These are the Kenites who came from Hammath, the father of the Rekabites." [1 Chronicles 2:55]

What's more? Jabez's blessings had a ripple effect to the extent that even his son Shallum became the king of Samaria. God's Word states that "Shallum son of Jabesh became king in the thirty-ninth year of Uzziah king of Judah, and he reigned in Samaria one month" [2 Kings 15:13].

God supernaturally granted Jabez's heart desire and honored him so much that even today people around the World remember him as a very prayerful Biblical figure. As a result, it makes Jabez's success story to be in alignment with the Word of God which states, "The LORD will make you the head, not the tail. If you pay attention to the commands of the LORD your God that I give you this day and carefully follow them, you will always be at the top, never at the bottom" [Deut, 28:13].

In another similar co-incidence, the Bible declares that, Patriarch Jacob's youngest son who was born to his favorite wife called Rachel. Benjamin's birth cost Rachel her life, so it makes it clear why Jacob's youngest son was very dear to him. Rachel named him Ben-Oni, *"son of my sorrow,"* in her suffering. But Jacob renamed him Benjamin meaning *"son of my right hand."* For it is written "Rachel was about to die, but with her last breath she named the baby Ben-Oni which means "son of my sorrow". The baby's father, however, called him Benjamin which means "son of my right hand"[Gen 35:18].

In the fullness of time, Benjamin was supernaturally blessed by God to the extent that he eventually became one of the twelve tribes in Israel.

Remember, Jabez was labeled with sorrow at birth by his mother. Likewise, Rachel also labeled her son with sorrow at birth, but Patriarch Jacob found it very necessary to rename his son.

In Biblical times, a person's name had a very significant meaning beyond giving names of relatives and famous people. The meaning behind the name often gave clue about the character. So, it is very significant to be extra careful to choose a befitting name for your children.

[Ref1 Nelson's New Illustrated Bible Dictionary Page 627]

Chapter 2

Jabez called on the God of Israel

NAMES OF GOD IN PRAYER

Jabez's call unto the God of Israel demonstrates how he prayed earnestly with confidence and sincerity for God to turn his situation around. The Bible declares, "Call onto Me and I will answer you, and I will tell you great and mighty things, which you do not know" [Jeremiah 33:3].

In those days, there were so many other gods in Israel but Jabez was specific to pray to the God of Israel. This shows that Jabez was a man of faith who knew Jehovah God. The Bible says, "but the people that do know their God shall be strong, and do exploits" [Daniel 11:32].

Prayer is very significant and very vital for believers because it is how we can communicate with the God of Israel and He also in turn communicates back to us. Therefore, it is a step in the right direction for Jabez to open his prayers by addressing the living God by His sovereign identity because He alone is worthy to receive that honor.

Again, Jabez demonstrated that he was a man of faith who backed up his prayers with strong petition to reach the throne room of God. The Bible tells us "let us therefore come boldly to the throne of grace, that we may obtain mercy and find grace to help in time of need" [Hebrews 4:16].

In ancient times, throughout the Scriptures, the living God revealed Himself to the Israelites through many names. God's names have special meanings and purposes attached to them. Jehovah God has many names and each one reveals Him in a very special way. In other words, God's names represent His nature and attributes. If God calls us by our names, then we are also entitled to address Him by His holy names.

Jesus Christ Himself taught mankind how to address God in our prayers this way "Our father in Heaven, Hallowed be Your name" [Matthew 6:9]. To hallow the name of God means to reverence His name with your whole heart and mind. Therefore, if we address God by His majestic names we demonstrate our humility and sincerity to trust Him alone for the purpose of our living.

How do you address God in your prayers? Is He your Most High God, God your great provider and your Abba Father? It is therefore very essential to address God by His majestic names for He alone deserves to be honored.

Furthermore, besides the God of Israel, the God of Abraham, Isaac and Jacob, there are so many other attributes of God that are mentioned in the Scriptures. Below are some of them:

[1] JEHOVAH-ROHI means "The Lord is my shepherd" [Psalms 23:1].

[2] ELOHIM means GOD. It is in reference to God's power and might. For it is written," In the beginning God created the heavens and the earth" [Genesis. 1:1].

[3] ADONAI meaning LORD. A reference to the leadership of God, The Scripture reveals, "A son honors his father, and a slave his master. If I am a father, where is the honor due me? If I am a master, where is the respect due me?" says the LORD Almighty" [Malachi 1:6].

[4] JEHOVAH-MACCADESHEM means the Lord who sanctifies you or the Lord who makes you holy. The Bible records, "But as for you, speak to the sons of Israel, saying, 'You shall surely observe My Sabbaths; for this is a sign between Me and you throughout your generations, that you may know that I am the LORD who sanctifies you." [Exodus 31:13].

[5] JEHOVAH-SHAMMAH means the Lord who is present, for it is written, "It was around about eighteen thousand measures: and the name of the city from that day shall be, The LORD is there" [Ezekiel 48:35].

[6] JEHOVAH-RAPHA meaning the Lord our healer. The Bible reminds us, "He said, if you listen carefully to the Lord your God, and do what is right in his eyes, if you pay attention to his commandments and keep all his decrees, I will not bring on you any of the deceases I brought on the Egyptians, for I am the LORD that heals you" [Exodus 15:26].

[7] JEHOVAH-TSIDKENU means the Lord our righteousness. For it is written "In his days Judah will be saved and Israel will live in safety. This is the name by which he will be called: The LORD Our Righteous Savior" [Jeremiah 23:6].

[8] JEHOVAH-JIREH means the Lord will provide. The Bible records

"Abraham looked up and there in a thicket he saw a ram caught by its horns. He went over and took the ram and sacrificed it as a burnt offering instead of his son. So, Abraham called that place The LORD Will Provide. And to this day it is said, on the mountain of the LORD it will be provided" [Genesis 22:13-14].

[9] JEHOVAH-NISSI means the Lord our Banner, The Bible states "Moses built an altar and called it The LORD is my Banner" [Exodus 17:15].

[10] JEHOVAH SHALOM means The Lord is peace. For it is written, "So Gideon built an altar to the LORD there and called it The LORD Is Peace. To this day it stands in Ophrah of the Abiezrites" [Judges 6:24].

[11] JEHOVAH SABBAOTH means the Lord of Hosts. As the prophet Isaiah records, "In the year that King Uzziah died I saw the Lord sitting upon a throne, high and lifted up; and the train of his robe filled the temple. Above him stood the seraphim. Each had six wings: with two he covered his face, and with two he covered his feet, and with two he flew. And one called to another and said: "Holy, holy, holy is the Lord of hosts; the whole earth is full of his glory!" [Isaiah 6:1-3].

[12] EL-SHADDAI means the Almighty God. The Bible reminds us, "When Abram was ninety-nine years old, the LORD appeared to him and said, "I am God Almighty; walk before me faithfully and be blameless" [Genesis 17:1].

[13] EL-OLAM means the Everlasting God. The Bible says that, "And Abraham planted a grove in Beersheba, and called there on the name of the LORD, the everlasting God" [Genesis 21:33].

[14] EL-ELYON meaning the Most Highest God. For it is written:

"After Abram returned from defeating Kedorlaomer and the kings allied with him, the king of Sodom came out to meet him in the Valley of Shaveh (that is, the King's Valley). Then Melchizedek king of Salem brought out bread and wine. He was priest of God Most High, and he blessed Abram, saying, "Blessed be Abram by God Most High, Creator of heaven and earth. And praise be to God Most High, who delivered your enemies into your hand" [Genesis 14:17].

[15] I AM WHO I AM was the sovereign identification name the Most High God gave to the prophet Moses. The Bible declares; Moses said to God, "Suppose I go to the Israelites and say to them, 'The God of your fathers has sent me to you,' and they ask me, 'What is his name?' Then what shall I tell them?" God said to Moses, "I AM WHO I AM. This is what you are to say to the Israelites: 'I AM has sent me to you.'" God also said to Moses, "Say to the Israelites, 'The LORD, the God of your fathers, the God of Abraham, the God of Isaac and the God of Jacob has sent me to you.' This is my name forever, the name you shall call me from generation to generation" [Exodus 3:14-15].

The Bible encourages believers to reverence God's excellent names. For it is written "O Lord our Lord, how excellent is Your name in all the earth" [Psalms 8:1].

The names and attributes of God point to certain functional capacities inherent in the nature of our God. When we are asking God to do something for us, we need to discover what name addresses our need. Remember that Jabez addressed God as the "God of Israel" in his open prayer and through that his prayers were answered. Therefore, it is very significant to emulate Jabez's worthy example.

Dear reader, I want to encourage you to take time to address God by using His various attributes; and also by concluding with the name which has been highly exalted above all names, in Heaven, on earth and under the earth, even in the holy name of Jesus Christ of Nazareth, the Son of the living God.

Chapter 3

Bless Me Indeed

GOD, THE GREAT PROVIDER

Jabez's first prayer point was to ask God, the great provider to bless him exceedingly or abundantly, The Bible declares. "The blessing of the LORD makes a person rich, and he adds no sorrow with it" [Proverbs 10:22].

A blessing is a special favor from Jehovah-Jireh. The blessing of God comes in two different dimensions, which are spiritual and natural provisions. As a result, God can supernaturally bless you with favors, responsibilities, influence, wisdom and knowledge if only you would avail yourself in prayers and hold on to His divine promises.

Perhaps, Jabez realized that it was only the blessings of God that could bring restoration upon his life so he requested for it and it was granted. The Bible reveals, "The Lord will make you abound in prosperity, in the offspring of your body and in the offspring of your beast and in the produce of your ground, in the land which the Lord swore to your fathers to give you" [Deuteronomy 28:11].

Dear reader, Jehovah-Jireh wants to bless you out of His riches in glory impelled by His love and mercy without your own effort if only you will be obedient to His word and pray earnestly.

Furthermore, blessing means, the act of declaring or wishing favor or wishing goodness over others. The blessing is not only good effect of words, it also has the power to bring them to pass.

For instance, the patriarchs pronounced blessings upon their children, often near death. Jehovah-Jireh blessed Abraham to become the father of many nations. The LORD said to Abraham "I will make you into a great nation, and I will bless you, I will make your name great, and you will be a blessing" [Genesis 12:2].

Father Abraham's son and grandson, Isaac and Jacob also received similar promises and became subject to the same covenants and obligations.

Therefore, after Abraham's death God poured out His manifold blessings upon Isaac. The Bible says: "And it came to pass after the death of Abraham, that God blessed his son Isaac; and Isaac dwelt by the well Lahairoi" [Genesis 25:11].

The Patriarch Isaac became a blessing to the children of Israel as he also passed it on to his son, Jacob. The Bible tells us that "So he came near and kissed him. And Isaac smelled the smell of his garments and blessed him and said, "See the smell of my son is as the smell of a field that the

Lord has blessed May God give you of the dew of heaven and of the fatness of the earth and plenty of grain and wine; Let peoples serve you, and nations bow down to you; Be Lord over your brothers, and may your mother's sons bow down to you. Cursed be everyone who curses you, and blessed be everyone who blesses you"[Genesis 27:27-29].

In fullness of time, Jacob was supernaturally blessed to the extent that he also became a blessing to the Israelites.

The more God blesses us the more He expects us to bless others. Blessing others has a ripple effect and therefore, our blessing should flow to others. For instance, it is in God's plan to bless us spiritually and naturally without our own efforts. God can bless His children with wealth, influence, favors, responsibilities, wisdom, and children or bless all our handy works so we can have a great impact in a society.

For instance, Joseph was richly blessed to the extent that every situation he found himself became a blessing to others. Captain Portipha's house was blessed because of Joseph his house keeper. For it is written, "The LORD was with Joseph so that he prospered, and he lived in the house of his Egyptian master. When his master saw that the LORD was with him and that the LORD gave him success in everything he did, Joseph found favor in his eyes and became his attendant. Portiphar put him in charge of his household, and he entrusted to his care everything he owned" [Genesis 39:2-4].

Following the same principle, blessing can be brought upon our workplace because of our presence of Godliness as Christians. Presumably, Jabez might have acknowledged the divine blessings of Jehovah Jireh bestowed upon the Patriarchs Abraham, Isaac, Jacob and the exploits of Joseph in Egypt which could have motivated him to tap into the supernatural blessings of God.

Remember, God blessed Jabez and he was more honorable for the city of Jabesh-Gilead to be named after him, apparently where the Scribes in Israel inhabited.

Jehovah Jireh has a complete plan for our lives to bless us if only we can pray earnestly and be obedient to His Word. For it is written "For I know the plans I have for you, declares the LORD, plans to prosper you and not to harm you, plans to give you hope and a future. Then you will call on me and come and pray to me, and I will listen to you. You will seek me and find me when you seek me with all your heart" [Jeremiah 29:11-12].

Again, God, our great provider, promises that when believers diligently seek Him with all their hearts they will find Him and His plans to prosper them will be fulfilled in their lives.

The Most High God answered Jabez's prayers to become a focal point for believers to learn a lesson from that shining example.

Therefore, it is imperative to emulate Jabez's prayer capabilities in order to tap into the supernatural blessings of God.

Chapter 4

Enlarge My Coast

GOD OF INCREASE

Jabez realized his limitations caused by a spoken curse so his second prayer point was to ask the God of increase to enlarge his coast. In other words, Jabez knew of his limitations so he asked God to increase his borders.

The "coast" literally means a boundary line between two nations which can also be referred to as territory. Likewise, every living soul has that mindset of coast or border enlargement as an inward desire. Therefore, "enlarge my coast" implies greater possession, greater authority and greater responsibility. For instance, when your coast is enlarged by the God of increase you will begin to experience the manifestation of a supernatural increase in your life. In other words, you might experience more favors, responsibilities, influence, and growth in all your handy works for you to make more impact in the society.

Dear reader, In the same vein, your ministry could be your borders and your business could also be your territory as well. Therefore, it is very significant to pray diligently for God to broaden your horizon in every dimension of your life.

Many a time, some believers think their success story or the increase they experience normally comes from their own efforts or hard work. The truth of the matter is that God works behind the scenes to replenish our resources. The Bible states that, "May the Lord made you increase and abound in love one another" [1 Thessalonians 3:12].

It is worthy to note that Jabez prayed for God to enlarge his coast. In other words, Jabez asked God for more favors, more opportunities, more responsibilities, to expand his sphere of influence and to broaden his scope. Later on, he experienced the divine blessings God had bestowed on him and as a result became the family head of a tribe in Judah(Ref1).

Eventually, Jabez was more honored with the city of Jabesh-Gilead, which was named after him. In other words, Jabez was tremendously blessed to the extent that he even became a blessing to the children of Israel.

As a believer, when a curse influences your blessings, you must, therefore, exercise your authority in Christ and pray to breakthrough barriers to expand your territory, then afterwards, "You shall remember the LORD your God, for it is He who gives you power to get wealth, that He may confirm His covenant that He swore to your fathers, as it is this day. [Deuteronomy 8:18]

For instance, the Scripture reveals to us about Noah "When he awoke from his drunken stupor he learned what his youngest son had done to him. So, he said, "Cursed be Canaan! The lowest of slaves he will be to his brothers." He also said, "Worthy of praise is the Lord, the God of Shem May Canaan be the slave of Shem. May God enlarge Japheth's territory and numbers" [Genesis 9:21-27a].

Patriarch Noah's confession of God to enlarge Japheth's territory ended up in a huge blessing to some great nations of the World.

Dear reader, presumably, you may be running a Church or a Bible school or a Charity organization or your own business such as farms, cattle rearing, homestead, sports club, soccer club, private school, shops, factories, transportations, assisted living, auto sales and many more. There is the need for you to pray diligently for God to enlarge your territory. The Bible makes it clear "Enlarge the place of your tent, stretch your tent curtains wide, do not hold back; lengthen your cords, strengthen your stakes" [Isaiah 54:2].

Therefore, it is my prayer that the Good Lord will bless you richly so as to expand your horizon in every department of your life as you meditate upon His Word.

[Ref 1 Nelson's New Illustrated Bible Dictionary Page 627]

Chapter 5

Your Hand Might Be With Me

THE HAND OF GOD

Jabez made a very strong petition through his third prayer point by asking 'the hand of God' to be upon his life. In other words, Jabez asked that God's hand would be with him to provide protection and divine guidance. The Bible records "fear not, for I am with you; be not dismayed, for I am your God; I will strengthen you, I will help you, I will uphold you with my righteous right hand" [Isa 41:10].

The 'hand of God' is a figure of speech which points to God's sovereign power. Just as a father lovingly guides his children so believers are also guided by the supernatural 'hand of God' behind the scene.

In other words, the expression 'hand of God' is symbolic of God's power and His presence to save in times of need. For it is written "Stretch out your hand to heal and perform signs and wonders through the name of your holy servant Jesus" [Acts 4:30].

You can also pray and ask God to stretch out His hands upon your life to bring you back on track when you find yourself in a very troubled situation.

The more believers acknowledge the 'hand of God' working on their behalf the better they will follow His lead. Therefore, believers can experience the 'hand of God' in their life like never before through studying of the Scriptures and praying without ceasing.

Again, the 'hand of God' is all that the believers need to overcome their difficult times so they can move forward in their Christian life. However, the 'hand of God' manifested spiritually for Jabez to taste the goodness of the Lord in his life so believers can also experience the same when they pray persistently.

Believers can experience the 'hand of God' in their lives if they humble themselves and walk in the light of His Word coupled with a powerful prayer life. Apostle Peter's exhortation to humility states that "Young men, in the same way be submissive to those who are older. All of you, clothe yourselves with humility toward one another, because, "God opposes the proud but gives grace to the humble." Humble yourselves, therefore, under God's mighty hand, that he may lift you up in due time. [1 Peter, 5:5-6]

As a believer, it is imperative to acknowledge the fact that God's hand is around you to lift you up when you are down and to strengthen you when you are weak.

Sometimes when we are going through trials and tribulations we are often unaware of God's hand guiding us. Years later, it becomes obvious how God supernaturally brought us through those difficult times. Looking back, we can testify about the 'hand of God' moving and guiding us to safety. The Bible teaches us that "Both riches and honor come from You, and You rule over all, and in Your hand is power and might; and it lies in Your hand to make great and to strengthen everyone" [1 Chronicles 29:12].

For instance, Joshua shared a powerful testimony to the children of Israel after they entered the promised land regarding the tremendous strength in the 'hand of God', For Joshua declared to the children of Israel, "He did this so that all the peoples of the earth might know that the hand of the LORD is powerful and so that you might always fear the LORD your God. [Joshua 4:24]

Presumably, Jabez acknowledged the fact that his broken life could only be fixed by the supernatural 'hand of God', hence, his prayer request asking for God's divine intervention. The Bible declares, "Though I walk in the midst of trouble, you preserve my life; you stretch out your hand against the wrath of my enemies, and your right hand delivers me. [Psalm 138:7]

Chapter 6

Keep Me From Evil

GOD, THE PROTECTOR

Jabez fourth prayer point was to ask God to protect him from evil so he can move forward. The Lord Jesus Himself taught us how to pray this way "And lead us not into temptation but deliver us from evil" [Matthew 6:13].

In other words, Jabez was expressing himself through prayer and in alignment with the Word of God which states "I am in pain and distress may your salvation O God protect me" [Psalm 69:29].

Certainly, Jabez acknowledged the fact that it was the evil one who exchanged his destiny with insufficiency coupled with grief. Thus, he prayed fervently to God not only to recover his destiny but also to protect him from the evil one. In other words, Jabez prayed that in receiving God's blessings he would not fall into temptation.

Therefore, in order to avoid falling into temptations, it is imperative to ask for God's protection through consistent and persistent prayers. For it is written "The Lord shall preserve you from all evil: He shall preserve your soul. The Lord shall preserve your going out and your coming in; from this time, forth and forevermore" [Psalm 121:7-8].

God protects His children in many diverse ways and sometimes we do not know how many times He rescues us from falling into temptation or from backsliding. However, in the world of freewill we make our own decisions, some of which are tough choices. Sometimes we make wrong choices without knowing it. As a result, God protects and safeguards us through the storms of life and lift us up from valleys as we pray consistently. King David the Psalmist said "The Lord is my shepherd: I shall not want. He makes me lie down in green pastures. He leads me beside the still waters. He restores my soul. He leads me in the path of righteousness for His name sake. Yeah, though I walk through the valley of the shadow of death, I will fear no evil" [Psalm 23:1-4].

Dear reader, when God's hand is upon your life it makes you secured; not to fear any evil and presumably that was why Jabez cried out to God for protection.

God has a perfect will for us so we can meditate upon His Word and pray without ceasing for His divine protection. The Bible declares, "He who dwells in the shelter place of the Most High will rest in the shadow of the Almighty. I will say of the Lord. He is my refuge and my fortress, my God, in whom I trust. Surely, He will save you from the fowler's snare and from the deadly pestilence. He will cover you with His feathers, and under His wings you will find refuge: His faithfulness will be your shield and rampart. You will not fear the terror of night, nor the arrow that flies by day, nor the pestilence that stalks in the darkness, nor the plague that destroys at midday" [Psalm 91:1-3].

God has promised us through the Scriptures regarding divine protection but we have to pray constantly to stay under His canopy. In other words, you have to be diligent in your prayers to stay under the shadow of God's wings. The Bible reminds us that, "No evil will befall you, Nor will any plague come near your tent" [Psalm 91:10].

For instance, before we became 'born again' we fell victim to temptations by the evil one. As a Christian too, there is the need to pray always not to yield to temptations. The Lord Jesus said, "Watch and pray so that you will not fall into temptation" [Matthew 26:41].

Again, as a believer, if per-adventure temptation befalls you, don't give up, but instead encourage yourself in the lord and persevere in prayers. The Good Lord will see you through those difficult times in accordance to His Word which states that "No temptations has overtaken you except what is common to mankind. And God is faithful; He will not let you be tempted beyond what you can bear. But when you are tempted, He will also provide a way out so that you can endure [1 Corinthians 10:13].

Certainly, it was the evil one who robbed Jabez of his more honorable status to become a 'nobody' in his household, but he prayed to God for his dignity to be restored and to be protected. In other words, Jabez recognized that his restoration will come with greater responsibility to resist temptation so he prayed for God's protection.

Chapter 7

That It May Not Grieve Me

GOD, THE DELIVERER

Don't let me experience the grief my name implies was the last prayer point of Jabez's encounter with God. The spoken curse over Jabez produced grief and insufficiency in his life. As a result, he needed deliverance to help him walk in the divine blessings of God.

Therefore, Jabez asked God to deliver him from a spoken curse which had been a thorn in his flesh. The Bible records, For He rescued us from the domain of darkness, and transferred us to the kingdom of His Beloved Son. [Colosians1:13]

In other words, every Christian is transformed to become a new creation in the Lord so as to break out from the past. Perhaps, before becoming a Christian you might have inherited some curses which might have influenced your blessings. So, it is very essential to pray and ask God to deliver you from any bondage.

Remember, Jabez's sorrowful and grieving situation occurred because of a spoken curse. However, Jabez self-deliverance prayer worked to perfection as God delivered him and granted him a double portion.

Another similar incident of spoken curse also occurred in the Scriptures. The Bible states, "And Noah awoke from his wine, and knew what his younger son had done unto him. And he said, cursed be Canaan; a servant of servants shall he be unto his brethren" [Genesis 9:24]. Eventually, this spoken curse ended up in affecting an entire human race.

The good news is that, this kind of curse can be nullified or broken by the blood of Jesus because of His finished work on the Cross of Calvary. For it is written, "Having canceled the charge of our legal indebtedness, which stood against us and condemned us; he has taken it away, nailing it to the cross" [Col 2:14].

One of the generational curses that sometimes have a toll on future generations is a spoken curse. Invariably, some curses might not be exactly the same as what Jabez inherited but rather in a different pattern.

For instance, there are families of today who are going through oppression, depression, addictions, unforgiving spirit, and terminal diseases like cancer due to generational curses. Some of these curses came about as a result of the sins of their forefathers. The Bible reminds us that "Our fathers have sinned, and are not, and we have borne their iniquity" [Lamentations 5:7].

Have you ever come across a family where the mother had a problem with excessive anger, his son seemed to have inherited that habit of which his grandma or grandpa had the same issue before? Such a consistent trend gives clear indication of generational curse operating in that particular family.

Therefore, it will interest you to know that there are so many generational curses out there such as fear, crime, lusts, miscarriage, hereditary sickness, financial insufficiency, accident prone, poverty, rejection, marital divorce and many more have been passed on from one generation to another.

Under the new covenant of God, the continual negative pattern of curses being handed down from one generation to another can be broken due to the finished work of Christ on the cross of Calvary. The Bible says "Surely he took up our infirmities and carried our sorrows: yet we considered him stricken by God, smitten by him, and afflicted. But he was pierced for our transgressions; he was crushed for our iniquities: the punishment that brought us peace was upon him, and by his wounds we are healed. We all like sheep have gone astray; each of us has turned to his own way, and the LORD has laid on him the iniquity of us all" [Isaiah 53:4-6].

The good news is that, the moment you accepted Jesus Christ as your personal savior and Lord, the transfer of curses from your forefathers to you stops henceforth. For the LORD Jesus was made a curse, so we can be freed from the curses that both our sins and those of our forefathers have brought upon us. The Bible makes it clear, "Christ has redeemed us from the curse of the law, being made a curse for us: As it is written, cursed is every one that hangs on a tree" [Galatians 3:13].

For this reason, it is very significant to pray persistently to break, renounce, revoke, reverse, avert and nullify all curses in the mighty name of Jesus and cast the demons out of your life. In fact, there is no obligation to be constantly breaking curses again and again.

Demons always look for a legal ground to operate because of the covenants entered into by the forefathers. For this reason, believers must be very careful about such things as unforgiving spirit, anger and bitterness. The Bible makes it plain that when we forgive others God will also forgive us (see Matthew 6:14-15), but when we harbor resentment in our hearts it will open the door for demons to operate against our soul and body.

The human composition consists of spirit, soul and body. It's the body which helps us to function in this physical World. The soul consists of the emotions (feelings), the will and the intellect (mind). It is the soul that helps a believer to put on the new life of the spirit through the renewing of the mind by the Word of God. The moment a person accepts Jesus Christ, only the spirit is re-created anew and set free automatically, but the soul and body can still be influenced by demons if they lead an ungodly lifestyle or if there be generational curses inherited from their forefathers. At this point, the person is not demon-possessed, but is said to be demon-influenced, usually with clear evidence of defeat and pain in his natural life.

However, such a believer needs to go through deliverance by using the authority Jesus gave us to take advantage of the freedom that He bought for us on the Cross of Calvary.

Above all, holiness must be the hallmark of every Christian in order not to open the door for demons to stage a comeback. For it is written: "Be holy, because I am holy" [1 Peter 1:16].

As a matter of fact, unbelievers are still affected by generational curses because they do not have Jesus Christ in their lives. In other words, generational curses are operating in the lives of those who are outside the new covenant of God.

Therefore, it is very crucial for unbelievers to give their lives to Jesus

Christ, the Son of the Living God in order to attain salvation and also to break away from generational curses. The Bible declares "Whoever believes in the Son has eternal life, but whoever rejects the Son will not see life, for God's wrath remains on them" [John 3:36].

Chapter 8

God Granted Jabez's Request

GOD ANSWERS PRAYERS

Jabez' desperate situation made him cry unto God for a divine intervention. God answered his travailing prayer to make it a very beautiful prayer masterpiece and inspiration for believers to emulate. God's Word tells us "Call to Me, and I will answer you, and show you great and mighty things you do not know" [Jeremiah 33:3].

In other words, Jabez's great expectation came through as he desperately prayed for a change and God granted him his heart's desire.

It also demonstrates that prayer has power to change your life and bring transformation upon you to impact your society like Jabez experienced.

This reveals that God answers prayers if only believers will pray diligently and hold unto His promises. So, it is of a great joy to see a miracle happen immediately after praying. The Bible reveals: "The righteous cry out, and the LORD hears them; he delivers them from all their troubles" [Psalm 34:17].

As a Christian, be encouraged to lift up your prayers to the next level. You need to be Spirit-filled so that the Holy Ghost will empower you to pray more effectively. The Bible says, "Likewise the Spirit also helps our infirmities: for we know not what we should pray for as we ought: but the Spirit itself makes intercession for us with groaning which cannot be uttered" [Romans 8:26].

The beauty of prayer is to get results from God and it does not depend on your eloquence, self-righteousness or being sanctimoniously religious person. But the beauty of your prayers depends upon what God will do immediately after you have prayed. The result is the most important thing and that was exactly what Jabez encountered after he prayed fervently.

Therefore, it is very significant for believers to emulate Jabez's prayer capabilities so as to build a relationship with God and abide in Him. The lord Jesus said, "If you abide in Me, and My words abide in you, you will ask what you desire, and it shall be done for you" [John 15:7].

Obviously, that is the confidence we have in drawing nearer to God, that if we ask anything according to His will, He listens to us. Therefore, if God listens to us, we know that we have whatever we ask of Him. The Scripture reveals: "This is the confidence we have in approaching God; that if we ask anything according to His will, He hears us. And if we know He hears us whatever we ask-we know that we have what we ask of Him." [1 John 5:14-15]

Dear reader, when God answers your prayers He puts a new song in your mouth so many people will hear to give Him all the glory and surrender to Him. King David said "He put a new song in my mouth, a song of praise to our God. Many will see and fear, and put their trust in the Lord. [Psalm 40:3]

Christians usually share their testimonies openly whenever God answers their prayers so that people will acknowledge God's glory and put their trust in Him.

Chapter 9

Lessons from Jabez's Prayer

FOOD FOR THOUGHT

Jabez's prayer encounter teaches us how to pray diligently with confidence in order to reach the throne room of God. Apparently, it will embolden believers to become prayer warriors or intercessors in their various capacities in the Ministry as God intended for His children to become. For it is written, "I urge, then, first of all, that petitions, prayers, intercession and thanksgiving be made for all people" [1Timothy 2:1].

Christians rely on Scriptures as their source of revelation about Jehovah God; therefore, they stand upon God's promises and persevere in prayers. The Bible makes it clear that "if my people, who are called by my name, will humble themselves and pray and seek my face and turn from their wicked ways, then I will hear from heaven, and I will forgive their sin and will heal their land" [2 Chronicles 7:14].

Again, Christians. are born winners so if Jabez's spiritual warfare worked to perfection then believers have the hope to follow up his worthy example.

What's more? Jabez's encounter also encourages us to eschew negative tendencies and to make positive confessions of God's Word into our situations so our ways would be prosperous. We are told in [1 Chronicles 4:9], that his mother called "Jabez", meaning "sorrow". But Jabez's positive confession in prayer changed his destiny. The Bible declares "The tongue has the power of life and death, and those who love it will eat its fruit" [Proverbs, 18:21].

True Biblical warfare is to find Scripture verses with a promise like salvation, protection, divine guidance, divine health, healing, favor, good success just to mention a few, which correspond to the situation one is dealing with, and to use those scripture promises to address the challenges by positive confession.

For instance, Apostle Peter described God's Word "incorruptible" seed which literally means incapable of dying. The Bible records "having been born again, not of corruptible seed, but of incorruptible, through the word of God, which lives and remains forever" [1 Peter 1:23].

The living Word of God is alive, sharper, and extremely powerful. The Bible tells us that, "For the word of God is alive and active. Sharper than any double-edged sword, it penetrates even to dividing soul and spirit, joints and marrow; it judges the thoughts and attitudes of the heart" [Hebrew 4:12].

Therefore, it is very significant to declare God's Word into your life so it can prosper your ways. Believing, thinking, and making a positive confession of God's Word goes together. God's Word teaches us that "As a man thinks so he is" [Proverbs 23:7].

Dear reader, you must think positively, believe right, and confess positively of God's Word concerning your situation.

As a result, I would like to encourage you to eschew negative confessions and start declaring God's Word into your situation so you can move forward in your Christian life.

Your confessions of God's Word are like a seed which will produce fruits, and your fruit will produce harvest. So, you must confess the Word of God and He will hasten His Word to perform it in your life [see Jeremiah 1:12]. The Bible teaches us that, "A man shall be satisfied with good by the fruit of his words, And the deeds of a man's hands will return to him" [Proverb 12:14].

In other words, your hands and mouth are working together to bring forth a harvest. For instance, if you are speaking words like poverty and destruction, your hands can not produce any blessings out of those negative utterances.

Furthermore, if you speak negative words, doubt and unbelief, God will not change your words but it is up to you to change your attitude by renewing of your mind by the Word of God. As it is written, "Do not conform to the pattern of this world, but be transformed by the renewing of your mind. Then you will be able to test and approve what God's will is--his good, pleasing and perfect will" [Romans 12:2].

Remember, Zechariah, the father of John the Baptist, when the angel of the Lord appeared to him (see Luke 1:5-20). He began to question God's Word sent by the angel. God had to shut his mouth so that he would not hinder the blessing God was trying to bring unto his life. Again, he told the angel of the Lord, "I am too old and my wife is also too old", meaning this just can't happen to me. The angel said I bring words from God for I stand in His presence and you will not be able to speak until the day God has fulfilled the promise to you, Zachariah.

Therefore, it is imperative to confess positive affirmations of God's Word into your situations to prosper your ways. The Bible states, "Do not let this Book of the Law depart from your mouth; meditate on it day and night, so that you may be careful to do everything written in it. Then you will be prosperous and successful" [Joshua 1:8].

Dear reader, you would realize that Jabez's prayer petition to the God of Israel yielded positive results as God granted his request. This gives believers the confidence that God answers prayers so all that believers have to do is to walk in the light of His Word coupled with prayer and expect the results. For it is written, "Therefore, I tell you, whatever you ask in prayer, believe that you have received it, and it will be yours." [Mark 11:24]

Finally, I would like to encourage you to walk with positive mental attitude, confess positively God's Word and inculcate the habit of praying in order to re-position yourself for God's unmerited favor.

Chapter 10

Solutions to Situations

GOD'S PROMISES

Jabez was designated to be more honorable than his brothers but a spoken curse influenced his blessings. However, he prayed fervently to break through those barriers for him to experience God's divine blessings. The Bible teaches us that, "No weapon that is formed against you shall prosper; and every tongue which rises against you in judgment you shall condemn. This is the heritage of the servants of the LORD, and their righteousness is of me, says the LORD" [Isaiah54:17].

In the same vein, one could also assume that some believers might have been favored by God but some curses surrounding their childbirth have adversely affected their blessings.

In other words, perhaps some believers could have been designated to be more honorable in their household or in the society. Perhaps, they could have been honorable statesmen or prominent persons in future but some negative influences emanating from their ancestral curses might have deprived them from fulfilling their destiny.

The good news is that, Jabez's fervent prayer breakthrough has become a focal point to encourage believers to become prayer warriors. The Bible declares, "For the weapons of our warfare are not carnal, but mighty through God to the pulling down of stronghold" [2 Corinthians 10:4].

Under the new covenant of God, Christians are justified by the blood of Jesus to revoke, renounce or to break curses in their lives. The Bible tells us that "When you were dead in your sins and in the uncircumcision of your flesh, God made you alive with Christ. He forgave us all our sins, having canceled the charge of our legal indebtedness, which stood against us and condemned us; he has taken it away, nailing it to the cross. And having disarmed the powers and authorities, he made a public spectacle of them, triumphing over them by the cross" [Colossians 2:13-15].

Therefore, Jabez's encounter reveals to us how to stand upon God's promises and to make a strong petition through prayer. In other words, believers are encouraged to confess the promises of God to address their situations in prayers so as to experience the supernatural blessings of God.

So, it is worthy to know the promises of God and quote them to address your situation in your daily prayers. The reason is that; God's Word contains literally thousands of His divine promises waiting to be claimed by faith through prayers. For it is written "For as many as are the promises of God, in Him they are yes; therefore, also through Him is our Amen to the glory of God through us" [2Corinthians 1:20].

Dear reader, it is my prayer that your faith and trust in God will be increased as you seek His face to supply your needs according to His riches in glory. The lists below are some of the promises of God available for you to claim by faith through prayers.

[1] In Times of Trouble

- Though I walk in the midst of trouble, you preserve my life; you stretch out your hand against the wrath of my enemies, and your right hand delivers me. [Psalm 138:7]

- The LORD is a refuge for the oppressed, a stronghold in times of trouble. [Psalm 9:9]

- And call upon me in the day of trouble: I will deliver you, and you shall glorify me. [Psalms 50:15]

- No temptation has overtaken you except what is common to mankind. And God is faithful; he will not let you be tempted beyond what you can bear. But when you are tempted, he will also provide a way out so that you can endure it. [1 Corinthians 10:13]

- When the righteous cry for help, the LORD hears and delivers them out of all their troubles. [Psalms 34:17]

- But you, O God, do see trouble and grief; you consider it to take it in hand. The victim commits himself to you; you are the helper of the fatherless. [Psalm 10:14]

- God is our refuge and strength, a very present help in trouble. [Psalm 46:1]

[2] Divine Protection

- He who dwells in the shelter of the Most High will abide in the shadow of the Almighty. I will say to the LORD, "My refuge and my fortress, my God, in whom I trust." For he will deliver you from the snare of the fowler and from the deadly pestilence.

- The angel of the LORD encamps around those who fear him, and he delivers them. [Psalms 34:7]

- For you have been my refuge, a strong tower against the foe. [Psalms 61:3]

- The LORD is my rock, my fortress, and my deliverer; my God is my rock, in whom I take refuge. He is my shield and the horn of my salvation, my stronghold. [Psalms 18:2]

- The name of the LORD is a strong tower: the righteous runs into it, and is safe. [Proverbs 18:10]

- My God, my rock, in whom I take refuge, my shield, and the horn of my salvation, my stronghold and my refuge, my savior; you save me from violence. I call upon the LORD, who is worthy to be praised, and I am saved from my enemies. [2 Samuel 22:3-4]

- The LORD will keep you from all evil; he will keep your life. The LORD will keep your going out and your coming in from this time forth and forevermore. [Psalms 121:7-8]

[3] Divine Guidance

- I will instruct you and teach you in the way you should go; I will counsel you with my loving eye on you. [Psalms 32:8]

- I am with you and will watch over you wherever you go, and I will bring you back to this land. I will not leave you until I have done what I have promised you." [Genesis 28:15]

- Trust in the Lord with all your heart and lean not on your own understanding: in all your ways submit to him, and he will make your paths straight [Proverbs 3:5-6]

- "They will not hunger or thirst, nor will the scorching heat or sun strike them down; For He who has compassion on them will lead them and will guide them to springs of water. [Isaiah 49:10]

- For thus says the Lord GOD, "Behold, I Myself will search for My sheep and seek them out. "As a shepherd cares for his herd in the day when he is among his scattered sheep, so I will care for My sheep and will deliver them from all the places to which they were scattered on a cloudy and gloomy day". I will bring them out from the peoples and gather them from the countries and bring them to their own land; and I will feed them on the mountains of Israel, by the streams, and in all the inhabited places of the land. I will feed them in a good pasture, and their grazing ground will be on the mountain heights of Israel. There they will lie down on good grazing ground and feed in rich pasture on the mountains of Israel. "I will feed My flock and I will lead them to rest," declares the Lord GOD. I will seek the lost, bring back the scattered, bind up the broken and strengthen the sick; but the fat and the strong I will destroy. I will feed them with judgment. [Ezekiel 34:11-16]

- The mind of man plans his way, but the LORD directs his steps. [Proverbs 16:9]

- I will lead the blind by a way they do not know, in paths they do not know I will guide them. I will make darkness into light before them and rugged places into plains. These are the things I will do, And I will not leave them undone. [Isaiah 42:16]

- For the Lamb in the center of the throne will be their shepherd, and will guide them to springs of the water of life; and God will wipe every tear from their eyes. [Revelation 7:17]

- The LORD will guide you always; he will satisfy your needs in a sun-scorched land and will strengthen your frame. You will be like a well-watered garden, like a spring whose waters never fail. [Isaiah 58:11]

- The steps of a good man are ordered by the Lord: and he

delights in his way. [Psalm 37:23]

[4] Deliverance from Distress/ Depression

- Be merciful to me, O LORD, for I am in distress; my eyes grow weak with sorrow, my soul and my body with grief. [Psalm 31:9]

- Then they cried unto the LORD in their trouble, and he saved them out of their distresses. He brought them out of darkness and the shadow of death, and brake their bands in sunder. Oh that men would praise the LORD for his goodness, and for his wonderful works to the children of men! For he hath broken the gates of brass, and cut the bars of iron in sunder. [Psalms 107:13-16]

- The LORD is a refuge for the oppressed, a stronghold in times of trouble. Those who know your name trust in you, for you: Lord have never forsaken those who seek you. [Psalms 9:9-10]

- Heaviness in the heart of man makes him stoop: but a good word makes him glad. [Proverbs 12:25]

- Though the mountains be shaken and the hills be removed, yet my unfailing love for you will not be shaken nor my covenant of peace be removed, says the LORD, who has compassion on you. [Isaiah 54:10]

[5] Fear not

- "Fear not, little flock, for it is your Father's good pleasure to give you the kingdom. [Luke 12:32]

- And he answered, Fear not: for they that be with us are more than they that be with them. [2 Kings 6:16]

- Even though I walk through the valley of the shadow of death, I will fear no evil, for you are with me; your rod and your staff, they comfort me. [Psalm 23:4]

- For God has not given us a spirit of fear, but of power and of love and of a sound mind. [2 Timothy 1:7]

- The Lord is my light and my salvation; whom shall I fear? The Lord is the strength of my life; of whom shall I be afraid? [Psalm 27:1]

- Fear not; for I am with you: be not dismayed; for I am your God: I will strengthen you, I will help you, I will uphold you with my righteous right hand. [Isaiah 41:10]

- Have I not commanded you? Be strong and courageous. Do not be afraid; do not be discouraged, for the Lord your God will be with you wherever you go . [Joshua 1:9]

- For I am the LORD your God who takes hold of your right hand and says to you, Do not fear; I will help you [Isaiah 41:13

- Be strong and courageous. Do not be afraid or terrified because of them, for the LORD your God goes with you; he will never leave you nor forsake you. [Deuteronomy. 31:6]

- David also said to Solomon his son, "Be strong and courageous, and do the work. Do not be afraid or discouraged, for the LORD God, my God, is with you. He will not fail you or forsake you until all the work for the service of the temple of the LORD is finished. [1 Chronicles 28:20]

- When I am afraid, I will trust in you. In God, whose word I praise, in God I trust; I will not be afraid. What can mortal man do to me? [Psalm 56:3-4]

- Do not be afraid; you will not suffer shame. Do not fear disgrace; you will not be humiliated. You will forget the shame of your youth and remember no more the reproach of your widowhood. [Isaiah 54:4]

- Be not be afraid of those who kill the body but cannot kill the soul. Rather, be afraid of the One who can destroy both soul and body in hell. [Matthew 10:28]

- The LORD is with me; I will not be afraid. What can man do to me? [Psalm 118:6]

- There is no fear in love. But perfect love drives out fear, because fear has to do with punishment. The one who fears is not made perfect in love. I1 John 4:18]

- For you did not receive a spirit that makes you a slave again to fear, but you received the Spirit of sonship. And by him we cry, "Abba," Father. [Romans 8:15]

[6] Baptism of the Holy Ghost

- When the day of Pentecost came, they were all together in one place. Suddenly a sound like the blowing of a violent wind came from heaven and filled the whole house where they were sitting. They saw what seemed to be tongues of fire that separated and came to rest on each of them. All of them were filled with the Holy Spirit and began to speak in other tongues as the Spirit enabled them. [Acts 2:1-4]

- Jesus said, "and I tell you, ask, and it will be given to you; seek, and you will find; knock, and it will be opened to you. For every one that asks to receive; and the one who seeks finds; and to the one who knocks it will be opened. What father among you, if his son asks for bread, will give him a stone? Or if he asks for a fish, will instead of a fish give him a serpent? Or if he asks for an egg, will give him a scorpion? If you then, who are evil, know how to give good gifts to your children: how much more will the heavenly Father give the Holy Spirit to those who ask him" [Luke 11:9-10]

- But you shall receive power when the Holy Spirit comes on you and you will be my witnesses in Jerusalem, and in all Judea and in Samaria and to the ends of the earth. [Acts 1:8]

- And it shall come to pass in the last days, says God, I will pour out of my Spirit upon all flesh: and your sons and your daughters shall prophesy, and your young men shall see visions, and your old men shall dream dreams: And on my servants and on my handmaidens, I will pour out in those days of my Spirit; and they shall prophesy. [Acts 2:17-18]

- Then Peter said to them, "Repent, and let every one of you be baptized in the name of Jesus Christ for the remission of sins; and you shall receive the gift of the Holy Spirit. [39] For the promise is to you and to your children, and to all who are afar off, as many as the Lord our God will call". [Acts 2:38-39]

- For John baptized with water, but in a few days, you will be baptized with the Holy Spirit. [Acts 1:5]

- Turn you at my reproof: behold, I will pour out my spirit to you, I will make known my words to you. [Proverbs 1:23]

- For by one Spirit are we all baptized into one body, whether Jews or Gentiles, whether bond or free; and have been all made to drink into one Spirit. [1 Corinthians 12:13]

- Not by works of righteousness which we have done, but according to his mercy he saved us, by the washing of regeneration, and renewing of the Holy Ghost. [Titus 3:5]

- That the blessing of Abraham might come on the Gentiles through Jesus Christ; that we might receive the promise of the Spirit through faith. [Galatians 3:14]

- And they were all filled with the Holy Ghost, and began to speak with other tongues, as the Spirit gave them utterance. [Acts 2:4]

- Jesus answered, Verily, verily, I say unto thee, except a man be born of water and [of] the Spirit, he cannot enter into the kingdom of God. [John 3:5]

- Jesus said, "I am going to send you what my Father has

promised; but stay in the city until you have been clothed with power from on high." [Luke 24:49]

- John answered them all, "I baptize you with water. But one who is more powerful than I will come, the straps of whose sandals I am not worthy to untie. He will baptize you with the Holy Spirit and fire. [Luke 3:16]

- The Spirit of truth, the world cannot accept him, because it neither sees him nor knows him. But you know him; for he lives with you and will be in you. [John 14:17]

- While Peter was still speaking these words, the Holy Spirit came on all who heard the message. The circumcised believers who had come with Peter were astonished that the gift of the Holy Spirit had been poured out even on Gentiles. For they heard them speaking in tongues and praising God. [Acts 10:44-46]

- But the Helper, the Holy Spirit, whom the Father will send in my name, he will teach you all things and bring to your remembrance all that I have said to you. [John 14:26]

- And Peter said to them, "Repent and be baptized every one of you in the name of Jesus Christ for the forgiveness of your sins, and you will receive the gift of the Holy Spirit. [Acts 2:38]

- Likewise, the Spirit helps us in our weakness. For we do not know what to pray for as we ought, but the Spirit himself intercedes for us with groaning too deep for words. [Romans 8:26]

- If you love me, you will keep my commandments. And I will ask the Father, and he will give you another Helper, to be with you forever, even the Spirit of truth, whom the world cannot receive, because it neither sees him nor knows him. You know him, for he dwells with you and will be in you. [John 14:15-17]

- And we are witnesses to these things, and so is the Holy Spirit, whom God has given to those who obey him. [Acts 5:32]

- And now, Lord, look upon their threats and grant to your servants to continue to speak your word with all boldness, while you stretch out your hand to heal, and signs and wonders are performed through the name of your holy servant Jesus." And when they had prayed, the place in which they were gathered together was shaken, and they were all filled with the Holy Spirit and continued to speak the word of God with boldness. [Acts 4:29-31]

- For it is not you who speak, but the Spirit of your Father speaking through you. [Matthew 10:20]

- And do not get drunk with wine, for that is debauchery, but be filled with the Spirit. [Ephesians 5:18]

[7] Divine Health / Healing

- He was despised and rejected by men; a man of sorrows, and acquainted with grief and as one from whom men hide their faces, he was despised and we esteemed him not. Surely he has borne our grief's and carried our sorrows: yet we did esteemed him stricken, smitten by God, and afflicted. But he was pierced for our transgressions, he was crushed for our iniquities upon him was the chastisement that brought us peace, and with his wounds we are healed. [Isaiah 53:3-5]

- But to you that fear my name shall the Sun of righteousness arise with healing in his wings; and you shall go forth, and grow up as calves of the stall. [Malachi 4:2]

- But I will restore you to health and heal your wounds, declares the LORD. 'because you are called an outcast, Zion for whom no one cares' [Jeremiah 30:17]

- Is any sick among you? let him call for the elders of the church; and let them pray over him, anointing him with oil in the name of the Lord: And the prayer of faith shall save the sick, and the

Lord shall raise him up; and if he hath committed sins, they shall be forgiven him. [James 5:14-15]

- Heal me, O LORD, and I will be healed; save me and I will be saved, for you are the one I praise. [Jeremiah 17:14]

- The LORD will protect him and preserve his life; he will bless him in the land and not surrender him to the desire of his foes. The LORD will sustain him on his sickbed and restore him from his bed of illness. [Psalm 41:2-3]

- Praise the LORD, O my soul, and forget not all his benefits, who forgives all your sins and heals all your diseases, who redeems your life from the pit and crowns you with love and compassion. [Psalm 103:2-4]

- He said, "If you listen carefully to the voice of the LORD your God and do what is right in his eyes, if you pay attention to his commands and keep all his decrees, I will not bring on you any of the diseases I brought on the Egyptians, for I am the LORD, who heals you." [Exodus 15:26]

- My son, pay attention to what I say; listen closely to my words. Do not let them out of your sight, keep them within your heart; for they are life to those who find them and health to a man's whole body. [Proverbs 4:20-22]

- He himself bore our sins in his body on the tree, so that we might die to sins and live for righteousness; by his wounds you have been healed. [1 Peter 2:24]

- He sent his word, and healed them, and delivered them from their destructions. [Psalm 107:20]

[8] BREAKTHROUGH/JOB SEEKING

- Every good gift and every perfect gift is from above, and comes down from the Father of lights, with whom is no variableness, neither shadow of turning [James 1:17].

- I will go before you and will level the mountains; I will break down gates of bronze and cut through bars of iron. I will give you hidden treasures, riches stored in secret places, so that you may know that I am the LORD, the God of Israel, who summons you by name [Isaiah 45:2-3]

- But my God shall supply all your need according to his riches in glory by Christ Jesus. [Philippians 4:19]

- May the favor of the Lord our God rest on us; establish the work of our hands for us-- yes, establish the work of our hands. [Psalms 90:17]

- And I will do whatever you ask in my name, so that the Father may be glorified in the Son. [John 14:13]

- Until now you have not asked for anything in my name. Ask and you will receive, and your joy will be complete. [John 16:24]

- If any of you lacks wisdom, you should ask God, who gives generously to all without finding fault, and it will be given to you. [James 1:5]

- Ask the Lord of the harvest, therefore, to send out workers into his harvest field." [Matthew 9:38]

- For I know the plans I have for you," declares the LORD, "plans to prosper you and not to harm you, plans to give you hope and a future. [Jeremiah 29:11]

- I can do all things through Christ who strengthens me [Philippians 4:13].

- So, you will find favor and good repute In the sight of God and man. [Proverbs 3:4]

- Surely, LORD, you bless the righteous; you surround them with your favor as with a shield. [Psalm 5:12]

- But you, LORD, are a shield around me, my glory, the One who lifts my head high. [Psalm 3:3]

- The righteous shall flourish like the palm tree: he shall grow like a cedar in Lebanon. [Psalm 92:12]

[9] PRAYER PROMISES

- Hear me when I call, O God of my righteousness: you have enlarged me when I was in distress; have mercy on me, and hear my prayer. [Psalm 4:1]

- The LORD is far from the wicked: but he hears the prayer of the righteous. [Proverbs 15:29]

- And he spoke a parable to them to this end, that men ought always to pray, and not to faint; [Luke 18:1]

- I will therefore that men pray everywhere, lifting up holy hands, without wrath and doubting. [1 Timothy 2:8]

- As for me, I will call upon God; and the Lord shall save me. Evening, and morning, and at noon, will I pray, and cry aloud: and he shall hear my voice. [Psalms 55:16-17]

- And all things, whatsoever you shall ask in prayer, believing, you shall receive. [Matthew 21:22]

- Do not be anxious about anything, but in every situation, by prayer and petition, with thanksgiving, present your requests to God. 7 And the peace of God, which transcends all understanding, will guard your hearts and your minds in Christ Jesus. [Philipian4:6-7]

- If you abide in Me and My words abide in you, ask whatever you wish and it shall be done for you [John 15:7]

[10] WEAPONS OF WARFARE

- This is what the Lord says to you: "Do not be afraid or discouraged because of this vast army. For the battle is not yours, but God's" [2 Chron. 20:15]

- "Put on the full armor of God, so that you can take your stand against the devil's schemes. For our struggle is not against flesh and blood, but against the rulers, against the authorities, against the powers of this dark world and against the spiritual forces of evil in the heavenly realms. Therefore, put on the full armor of God, so that when the day of evil comes, you may be able to stand your ground, and after you have done everything, to stand. Stand firm then, with the belt of truth buckled around your waist, with the breastplate of righteousness in place, and with your feet fitted with the readiness that comes from the gospel of peace. In addition to all this, take up the shield of faith, with which you can extinguish all the flaming arrows of the evil one. Take the helmet of salvation and the sword of the Spirit, which is the word of God" [Eph. 6:11-17]

- Submit yourselves to God. Resist the devil, and he will flee from you." [James 4:7]

- "You are from God, little children, and have overcome them; because greater is He who is in you than he who is in the world." [1 John 4:4]

- "For though we live in the world, we do not wage war as the world does. The weapons we fight with are not the weapons of the world. On the contrary, they have divine power to demolish strongholds. We demolish arguments and every pretension that sets itself up against the knowledge of God, and we take captive every thought to make it obedient to Christ." [2 Cor. 10:3-5]

- "In all these things, we are more than conquerors through Him who loved us."[Romans. 8:37]

- "But thanks be to God, who gives us the victory through our Lord Jesus Christ." [1 Cor. 15:57]

- "Not by might nor by power, but by My Spirit,' says the Lord of hosts." [Zech. 4:6]

- "Behold, I have given you authority to tread on serpents and scorpions, and over all the power of the enemy, and nothing shall hurt you." [Luke 10:19]

- The thief comes only to steal and kill and destroy. I came that they may have life and have it abundantly." [John 10:10]

- "Truly I tell you, whatever you bind on earth will be bound in heaven, and whatever you loose on earth will be loosed in heaven. Again, truly I tell you that if two of you on earth agree about anything they ask for, it will be done for them by my Father in heaven." [Matt. 18:18-19]

- The Lord will cause your enemies who rise against you to be defeated before you. They shall come out against you one way and flee before you seven ways." [Deut. 28:7]

- And they have conquered him by the blood of the Lamb and by the word of their testimony, for they loved not their lives even unto death. [Rev.12:11]

- ....the reason the Son of God appeared was to destroy the devil's work. [1 John 3:8]

- "Do not fear them, for the Lord your God is the one fighting for you." [Deut. 3:22]

- "What then shall we say to these things? If God is for us, who is against us?" [Rom. 8:31]

- "For You have girded me with strength for battle; You have subdued under me those who rose up against me." [Psalm 18:39]

- "Through You we will push back our adversaries, through Your name we will trample down those who rise up against us." [Psalm 44:5]

- See, today I appoint you over nations and kingdoms to uproot and tear down, to destroy and overthrow, to build and to plant

[Jeremiah 1:10]

- You are my battle-axe and weapons of war: for with you will I break in pieces the nations, and with you will I destroy kingdoms; [Jeremiah 51:20]

- Blessed be the LORD my strength, who teaches my hands to war, and my fingers to fight: [Psalm 144:1]

- Let God arise, let his enemies be scattered: let them also that hate him flee before him. [Psalm 68:1]

- Arise, LORD, in your anger; rise up against the rage of my enemies. Awake, my God; decree justice. [Psalm 7:6]

- For our "God is a consuming fire" [Hebrews 12:29]

- Fire goes before him and consumes his foes on every side. [Psalm 97:3]

- Our God comes and will not be silent: a fire devours before him, and around him a tempest rages. [Psalm 50:3]

- For the LORD, your God is the one who goes with you, to fight for you against your enemies, to save you. [Deuteronomy 20:4]

- No weapon that is formed against you shall prosper; and every tongue that shall rise against you in judgment you shall condemn. This is the heritage of the servants of the LORD, and their righteousness is of me, says the Lord. [Isaiah 54:17]

- He trains my hands for battle; my arms can bend a bow of bronze. [Psalm 18:34]

- Out of the mouth of babes and suckling's have you ordained strength because of your enemies, that you might still the enemy and the avenger. [Psalm 8:2]

Beloved, the most beautiful part of Christianity is your right to talk to God directly through prayers. God answers prayers if even you sometimes do not have the words to say. You just speak from your heart and He will listen but it is very significant to read the Scripture verses regarding prayer so that you can draw closer to God. However, God's promises will teach you how to pour your heart out in words spontaneously. Therefore, you must always take time out of your day to have your devotion time and pray through God's promises.

Conclusion

One turning point every Christian is longing for is to move out of a troubled life to a successful living. Therefore, Jabez prayed fervently that his life might be both wealthy and healthy. The Bible declares, "Beloved, I pray that in all respects you may prosper and be in good health as your soul prospers." [3 John 1:2]

In life, naming a child is very significant, and it is one of the biggest events in human history since the time of Adam. Names have meanings which can define a child's character. In other words, names and the naming process are very crucial to determine the child's destiny in future.

Around the World naming ceremonies varies with its implications in a very diverse manner in terms of culture, tradition, and religion across the spectrum. Some traditions have even veered off the mark to deeply connect with idolatry which does not augur well for the children's future and must be declared outmoded. Therefore, it is imperative for believers to name their children according to the Christian principles in order to allow God's divine favor to shine over their lives.

For instance, in African tradition, especially, in Akan societies of West Africa, names, and the process of naming a child is very essential since everyone born into this World has a mission. Seven days exactly after the childbirth the process of naming the baby begins. During the baby naming ceremony, the immediate relatives, families, and friends rally together in their community which includes a linguist or a master of ceremony to perform the customary rites. However, the linguist pours the libation and after that he dips his forefinger into the liquor of alcohol and touches the child's tongue whiles mentioning the child's name. Again, the linguist dips his forefinger into a glass cup of water and touches the child's tongue or lips. Afterwards, the linguist makes some pronouncements over the child by saying 'if you say wine let it be wine' and 'if you say water let it be water' which literally means let your yes be yes and your no be no. On the contrary, the practice of necromancy and invocation of ancestral spirits during libation pouring is abomination unto the Most High God. For it is written "A charmer or a medium or a necromancer or one who inquires of the dead, for whoever does these things is an abomination to the LORD" [Deut 18:11-12]. Gradually, this kind of traditional naming rite is dwindling to a vanishing point due to the spread of Christianity in West Africa.

In this modern time, no committed Christian will compromise and allow libation to be poured during child naming ceremony. But before you gave your life to Christ who knows what actually transpired during your childbirth?

Maybe as an African during your naming ceremony libation was poured to signify your bright future but it has now turned back to influence your blessings. For this reason, the Bible makes it plain that, "Making the word of God of no effect through your tradition, which you have delivered: and many such things do you"[Mark 7:13].

Beloved, I have some good news for you; if Jabez was able to pray unto God to change his destiny for the better you can do the same through the shed blood of Jesus on the Cross of Calvary. For it is written "Blotting out the handwriting of ordinances, that was against us which was contrary to us, and took it out of the way, nailing it to His Cross" [Colossians 2:14].

Therefore, as a Christian, you must exercise your authority in Christ and tenaciously pray to break every curse in your life by the blood of Jesus.

Remember, Jabez literally means "sorrow" which influenced his more honorable character to become nobody but his name was changed when naming him after a city called Jabesh-Gilead.

The Most High God, Himself is very particular about names. For instance, God had to change Abram meaning 'Exalted father' to Abraham meaning 'Father of multitude of Nations' [see ref1]. The Bible records "No longer shall your name be called Abram, but your name shall be Abraham; For I will make you the father of a multitude of nations" [Genesis 17:5]. And it came to pass that Patriarch Abraham became the father of many nations for the whole World to acknowledge. If that be the case, then you must also consider the names you will choose for your children so as to bring God's blessings upon their lives in future.

As matter of fact, children are vulnerable so you must be careful of whom you name your kids after. Also, the environment and the upbringing can have influence on the kid's life. So, it is imperative to bring up your kids in the fear of the Lord and also in a good environment. The Bible teaches us that "train up a child in the way he should go, and when he is old he will not depart from it" [Proverbs 22:6].

As a Christian, be encouraged to name your children after some God-fearing family members and most significantly dedicate your children unto the Most High God.

Have you ever come across a situation where some parents or guardians made some negative pronouncements against their children? Some parents or guardians rely on negative language to address their children whenever they make mistakes. Perhaps, their perception is that negative utterance will make their children responsible. As such, they end up in making worse mistakes by saying negative things like "you are dumb" or "you are useless" or "you are good for nothing" or "you are a bad kid" or you will not achieve anything in life and what have you. This trend could have an adverse effect on the child's future if care is not taken

Dear reader, be encouraged to eschew negative confessions and always declare God's blessings over your children so that they will bear good fruits in future. The Bible makes it clear that. "Children are a heritage from the Lord, offspring a reward from Him" [Psalm 127:3].

Every person at a point in time has had negative things spoken over them in the past. Maybe someone told you that you are not going to be successful in life. It's almost like cursing your future. As a Christian, confidently exercise your spiritual authority and renounce every negative word spoken over you and break its power by the blood of Jesus.

Some nicknames could also have an adverse effect on a person's life. In life, some people choose to label their friends or even themselves with some negative nicknames, especially, after some horror movie stars or some violent movie actors such as, "Terminator", "Destroyer" or "Killer" and what have you. These negative nicknames could have a great impact on a person's life if care is not taken.

[Ref1 New Illustrated Bible Dictionary Page 8]

Quiz Program

Dear reader, if you read this book very carefully, you would be able to answer the following questions.

[1] What is the meaning of Jabez?

[2] What is the meaning of Ben-Oni?

[3] What is the meaning of Benjamin?

[4] What are the similarities between Jabez and Benjamin's birth scenario?

[5] What was the reason behind Petrarch Jacob's renaming Benjamin?

[6] How would you describe a spoken curse?

[7] Eventually, Jabez was named after which city in Israel?

[8] How many powerful prayer points did Jabez make?

[9] How did the Apostle Peter describe God's Word?

[10] Who redeemed mankind from the curse of the law?

[11] How would you describe the 'hand of God'?

[12] What is the significance of declaring God's Word into your life?

[13] Name some of the God's attributes that marches your needs?

[14] Whose name has been highly exalted above all names in Heaven, on earth and under the earth?

[15] Who empowers Christians to pray more effectively?

Notes

Notes

Notes

www.ingramcontent.com/pod-product-compliance
Lightning Source LLC
Chambersburg PA
CBHW021158080526
44588CB00008B/395